M000083990

This gift is for

_____

from

_____

TIME *for* MYSELF

Quiet Thoughts
For Busy Women

Janet M. Congo
Julie L. Mask
Jan E. Meier

A
JANET
THOMA
BOOK

THOMAS NELSON PUBLISHERS
Nashville

Published in Nashville, Tennessee, by
Thomas Nelson, Inc., and distributed in
Canada by Lawson Falle, Ltd., Cambridge,
Ontario.

Scripture quotations are from the NEW
KING JAMES VERSION of the Bible.
Copyright © 1979, 1980, 1982, Thomas
Nelson, Inc., Publishers.

Library of Congress Number: 92-51007
Printed in Hong Kong.
1 2 3 4 5 6 — 98 97 96 95 94 93

Be still and know
that I am God.
—Psalm 46:10

If our life is never quiet,
we starve spiritually. A
sense of peace and purpose
is the result of living life
from the inside out.

I will say of the LORD,
"He is my refuge and
my fortress;
My God, in Him I
will trust."
—Psalm 91:2

Stress comes when we feel alone in the midst of pressure. God offers a refuge. If we take time out to turn to Him, we need not go through the storms of life alone.

And whatever you do,
do it heartily, as to the
Lord and not to men.
—Colossians 3:23

We sometimes become
blinded to the folly of
trying too hard to please
other people. If we live for
the approval of God, rather
than that of other people,
we will be richly rewarded.

Therefore, putting away lying, "Let each one speak truth with his neighbor," for we are members of one another.
—Ephesians 4:25

Many of us have
learned to avoid speaking
the truth in order to keep
peace. We need to
remember that honesty
can be practiced with
kindness and love.

Do not let your
adornment be merely
outward . . . but let it be
the hidden person of the
heart, with the
incorruptible beauty of a
gentle and quiet spirit,
which is very precious in
the sight of God.
—1 Peter 3:3–4

Excessive focus on our outward beauty results in our veiling the hidden beauty that is our true asset. Letting people know the real person behind the mask takes courage and trust in God. It is the only way to true intimacy.

Now godliness with
contentment is great gain.
—1 Timothy 6:6

Many things may bring
us pleasure, but unless we
are content, nothing fulfills
us. Contentment occurs
when we are at peace with
God and ourselves.

He gives power
to the weak,
And to those who
have no might
He increases strength.
—Isaiah 40:29

In order for us to find
peace, we must realize we
are powerless and let God
provide the daily power
to walk through
another battle.

You have hedged me
behind and before,
And laid Your hand
upon me.
—Psalm 139:5

We need to set limits
and create personal
boundaries to protect areas
of self that should not be
usurped by others.
Although people may not
always respect our
boundaries, God hedges
our souls for eternity with
the boundary of His
never-failing love.

Who shall separate us
from the love of Christ?
—Romans 8:35

Even when we feel as
if God is distant, He
continues to look at us
with eyes of compassion
and love, with no
condemnation in His gaze.
He sees each of us as a
highly significant woman.

It is vain for you
to rise up early,
To sit up late.
—Psalm 127:2

Rest is so important for human beings that God made it the basis of the Fourth Commandment. It's part of His plan for even the most accomplished woman.

A word fitly spoken is
like apples of gold
In settings of silver.
—Proverbs 25:11

Words are so powerful.
They can be used to
encourage, affirm, and
build up or they can tear
down, discourage, and
destroy. The choice is ours.

Therefore we do not lose heart. Even though our outward man is perishing, yet the inward man is being renewed day by day.
—2 Corinthians 4:16

Even as I face physical changes and limitations, I can be growing stronger in my heart and soul. As I fill my mind with God's Word, pray, and meditate, I am renewed. God grows in me an inner quietness and strength.

I have learned in
whatever state I am,
to be content.
—Philippians 4:11

Contentment is the natural result of being rooted and grounded in Christ's love. The winds of life may continue to whirl about you, but in your core self you can be at rest in Jesus' loving arms.

Through the LORD's
mercies we are not
consumed,
Because His compassions
fail not.
They are new every
morning;
Great is your faithfulness.
—Lamentations 3:22–23

God in His mercy
provided a way for us to
get to Heaven without
having to be perfect. His
mercy, compassion, and
faithfulness continue
toward us in spite of
our shortcomings.

He who dwells in
the secret place of
the Most High
Shall abide under the
shadow of the Almighty.
I will say of the LORD,
"He is my refuge and
my fortress;
My God, in Him I
will trust."
—Psalm 91:1–2

Find God's secret place
to dwell—an intimate,
moment-by-moment
relationship with Him.

Blessed are the
peacemakers,
For they shall be called
sons of God.
—Matthew 5:9

Peacekeepers see conflict as the ultimate enemy and will do anything to avoid it. Peacemakers, by contrast, see conflict as an opportunity to gain understanding by honestly looking at differences.

Casting all your care
upon Him, for He
cares for you.
—1 Peter 5:7

Jesus Christ doesn't deal with us from afar. He comes alongside us to express His care. We don't have to become more spiritual to reach Him. He became human to touch us.

A man [woman] of great
wrath will suffer
punishment;
For if you rescue him, you
will have to do it again.
—Proverbs 19:19

Sometimes we have been trained to accept other people's feelings as our responsibility. This keeps others from accepting their own responsibility. Pray for wisdom to know what is yours and what is theirs.

Now this is the
confidence that we have
in Him, that if we ask
anything according to His
will, He hears us.
—1 John 5:14

Thank you, Lord, that
you are even more willing
to answer my prayer than
I am to ask.

And Jesus answered and said to her, "Martha, Martha, you are worried and troubled about many things. But one thing is needed, and Mary has chosen that good part, which will not be taken away from her."
—Luke 10:41–42

Lord, help me remember
that relationship is more
important than reputation.

Whatever you do in word or deed, do all in the name of the Lord Jesus, giving thanks to God the Father through Him.
—Colossians 3:17

Every calling—even to
housework—is a holy
calling if I'm doing it
for the Lord.

As iron sharpens iron,
So a man sharpens the
countenance of his friend.
—Proverbs 27:17

In a healthy growing relationship, both partners are enhanced rather than absorbed. Autonomy often just binds people to their own smallness.

So God created man in
His own image; in the
image of God He created
him; male and female
He created them.
—Genesis 1:27

God didn't create
human beings to blend in
with their surroundings.
He made each of us
unique.

And I was afraid, and
went and hid Your talent
in the ground.
—Matthew 25:25

How often we crucify
ourselves between two
thieves: regret for yesterday
and fear of tomorrow.
Avoiding failure is a waste
of life. Seeking success is
a better choice.

For where envy and
self-seeking exist,
confusion and every evil
thing will be there.
—James 3:16

Many of our seemingly admirable efforts are really attempts to earn praise and feel loved. God, not other people, is the only dependable source of love. Confusion vanishes in the light of the truth of His unconditional love.

And a great windstorm
arose . . . But [Jesus] was
in the stern, asleep on the
pillow. And they awoke
Him and said to Him,
"Teacher, do You not care
that we are perishing?"
—Mark 4:37–38

One of the worst things about a crisis is that awful feeling of being out of control. Calmness in crisis is a direct result of concentrating on God's closeness and care. We fear too much because we trust too little.

When I kept silent, my
bones grew old
Through my groaning all
the day long.
—Psalm 32:3

Because of fear of rejection, some women endure dark pain alone. The silent hurts must be courageously exposed in order to find healing.

Praying always with all prayer and supplication in the Spirit, being watchful to this end with all perseverance and supplication for all the saints.
—Ephesians 6:18

Asking why in the midst of trials leads to more confusion, whereas asking how leads to greater reliance on Christ, and with it, a way through the storm.

Let no one despise you.
—Titus 2:15

To the best of our ability, we must refuse to let ourselves be sexually, physically, or verbally abused. Our body is a temple of the Holy Spirit, so we have a duty to protect ourselves.

For as he thinks in his
heart, so is he.
—Proverbs 23:7

Self-defeating cycles can
be broken, but only if the
heart is touched at an
emotional and thinking
level. That happens if,
every day, we dedicate
our minds and our
thoughts to Jesus.

If we confess our sins, He is faithful and just to forgive us our sins and to cleanse us from all unrighteousness. If we say that we have not sinned, we make Him a liar, and His word is not in us.
—1 John 1:9–10

It can be scary to admit our mistakes and imperfections, yet only when we are willing to risk such vulnerability can we experience God's cleansing and healing power at work.

For you, brethren, have
been called to liberty; only
do not use liberty as an
opportunity for the flesh,
but through love serve
one another.
—Galatians 5:13

Whether we are serving
each other in love or
merely acting as a martyr
depends on our inner
motive. What
is yours?

Speaking the truth
in love.
—Ephesians 4:15

We often associate speaking the truth with criticism, verbal abuse, or sarcasm. We need to learn that when expressed lovingly and constructively, honesty builds other people up.

God is able to make all
grace abound toward you,
that you . . . may have an
abundance for every
good work.
—2 Corinthians 9:8

God hasn't promised a
life without trials, but He
has promised us grace
for the journey.

For He satisfies the
longing soul,
And fills the hungry soul
with goodness.
—Psalm 107:9

Happiness is a brief
emotion that comes and
goes, but contentment
endures. It is our faith
rather than life experience
that produces true
contentment.

Call upon Me in
the day of trouble;
I will deliver you, and
you shall glorify Me.
—Psalm 50:15

You can't overcome your troubles without God's help. Call on Him. He loves you and wants to deliver you from trouble.

For whatever things were
written before were written
for our learning, that we
through the patience and
comfort of the Scriptures
might have hope.
—Romans 15:4

The key to being able to hope in God is to confront what caused us to lose hope in the first place. Although there are those in this world who are not safe to put our hope in, God is always a dependable source of hope.

For I will forgive their
iniquity, and their sin I will
remember no more.
—Jeremiah 31:34

It is easy to waste energy
on regrets, but God invites
us to tenderly release our
regrets through confession,
freeing us to use our
energy on growth.

Put my tears into
Your bottle;
Are they not in Your book?
—Psalm 56:8–9

God knows and understands your deep pain. He loves you so intimately and considers you so important that He even keeps track of your tears.

Whoever listens to
me will dwell safely,
And will be secure,
without fear of evil.
—Proverbs 1:33

Life's storms are inevitable, yet unpredictable. We don't know how they will change our lives. If we fight the urge to panic, God's powerful presence will dissolve our fears.

Now may the God of
patience and comfort grant
you to be like-minded
toward one another,
according to Christ Jesus.
—Romans 15:5

Patience is a part of accepting who we are and being satisfied with how we have been created—as growing individuals with whom God is not yet finished. We often run from ourselves to avoid facing this fact.

The thief does not come except to steal, and to kill, and to destroy. I have come that they may have life, and that they may have it more abundantly.
—John 10:10

The "thief"—Satan—
delights when we
lose hope, question
God, or dwell on
our inadequacies.
He is defeated through
God's grace, given flesh by
Jesus Christ, who always
affirms our value.

"Be angry and do not
sin": do not let the sun go
down on your wrath.
—Ephesians 4:26

God invites us to
express all of our feelings
to Him—even our anger
and fear. He desires
honesty in our innermost
being.

Faithful are the wounds
of a friend,
But the kisses of an enemy
are deceitful.
—Proverbs 27:6

With certain individuals,
our best defense is to pray
for them and remove our
vulnerability. Try to discern
friends from enemies.

Therefore whoever humbles himself as this little child is the greatest in the kingdom of heaven.
—Matthew 18:4

It will always be necessary to protect ourselves from some things in the world. If we are going to grow closer to God, however, we must approach Him with the trusting spirit of a little child.

That we may lead a quiet
and peaceable life in all
godliness and reverence.
—1 Timothy 2:2